Hi there, my name is Jeff.
I hope you enjoy this coloring book.

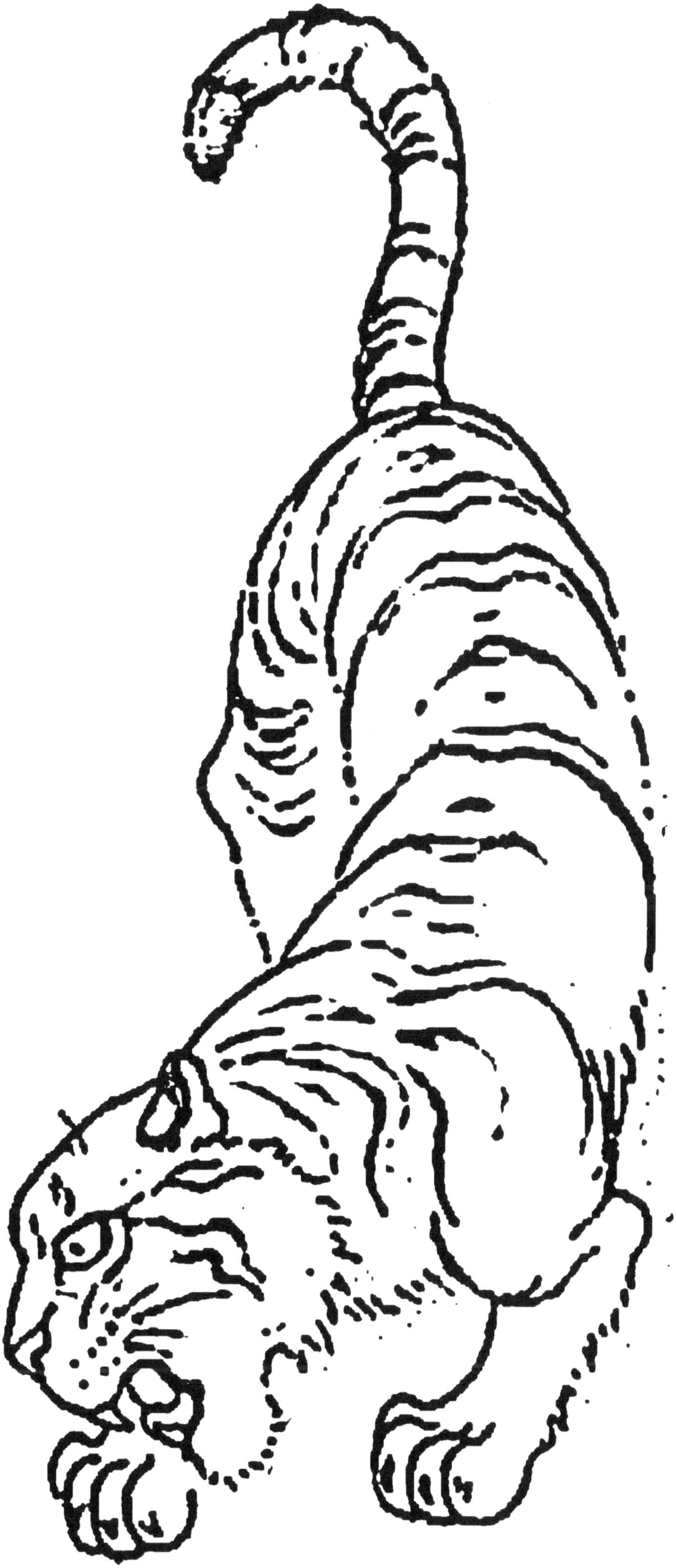

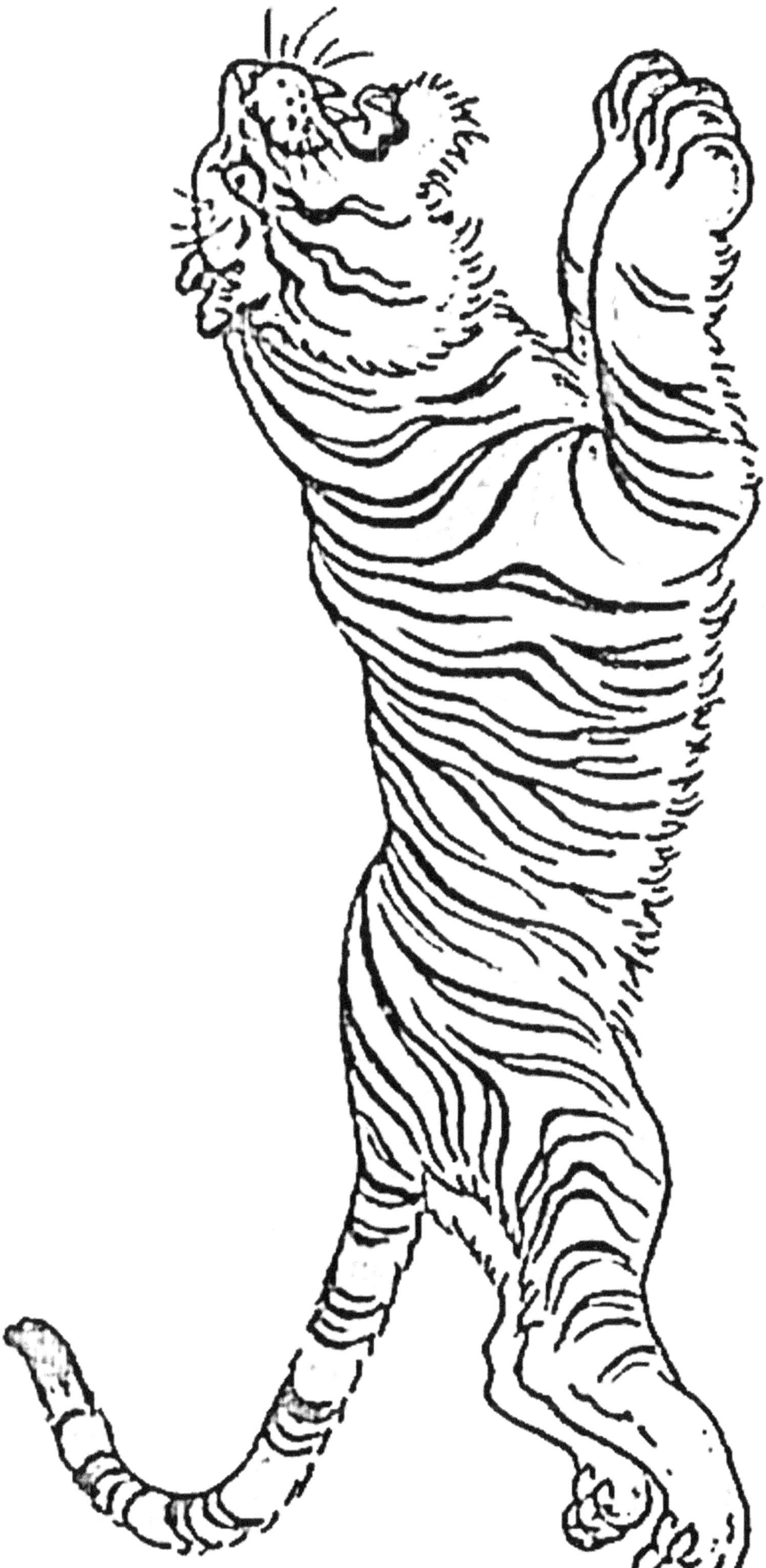

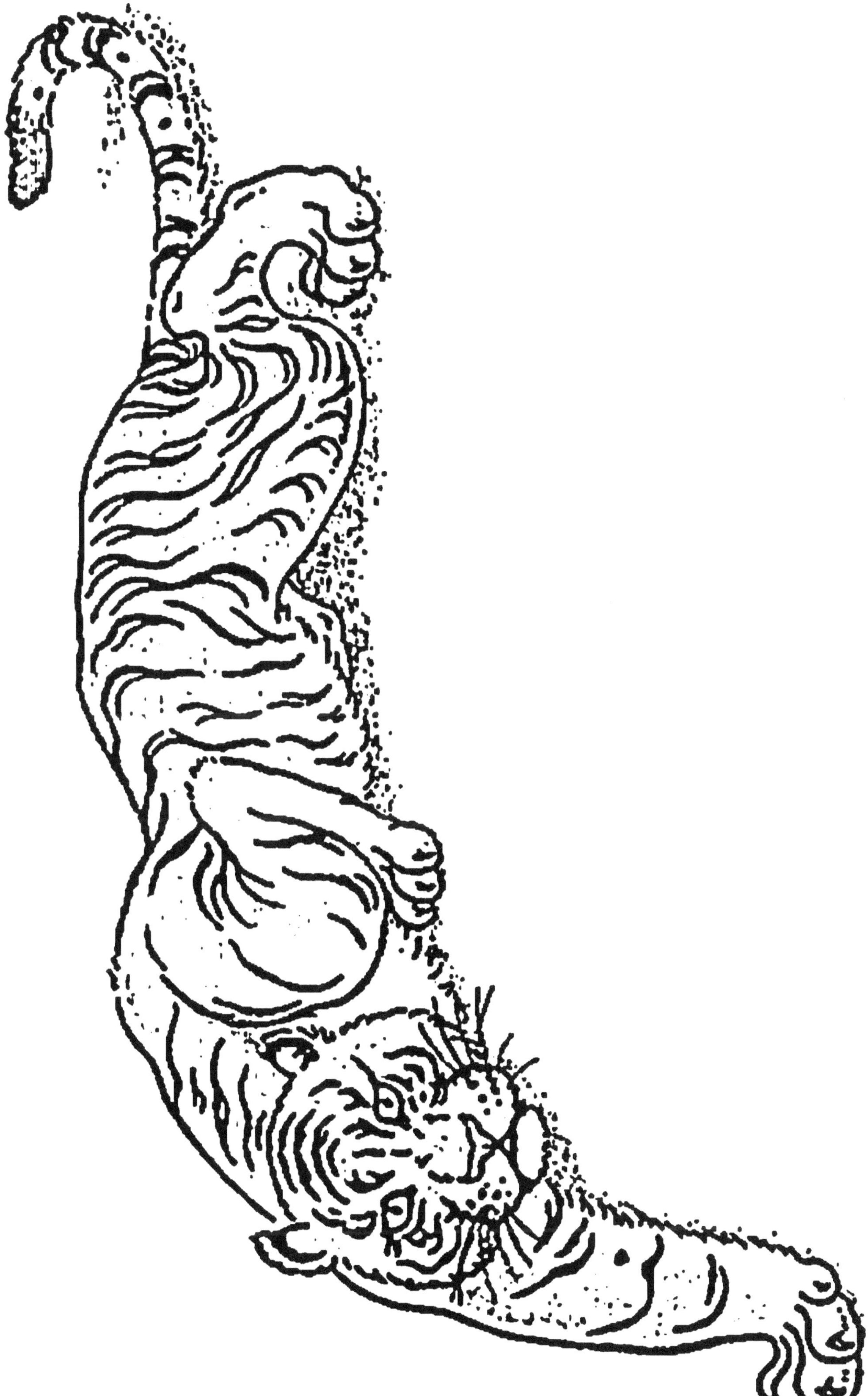

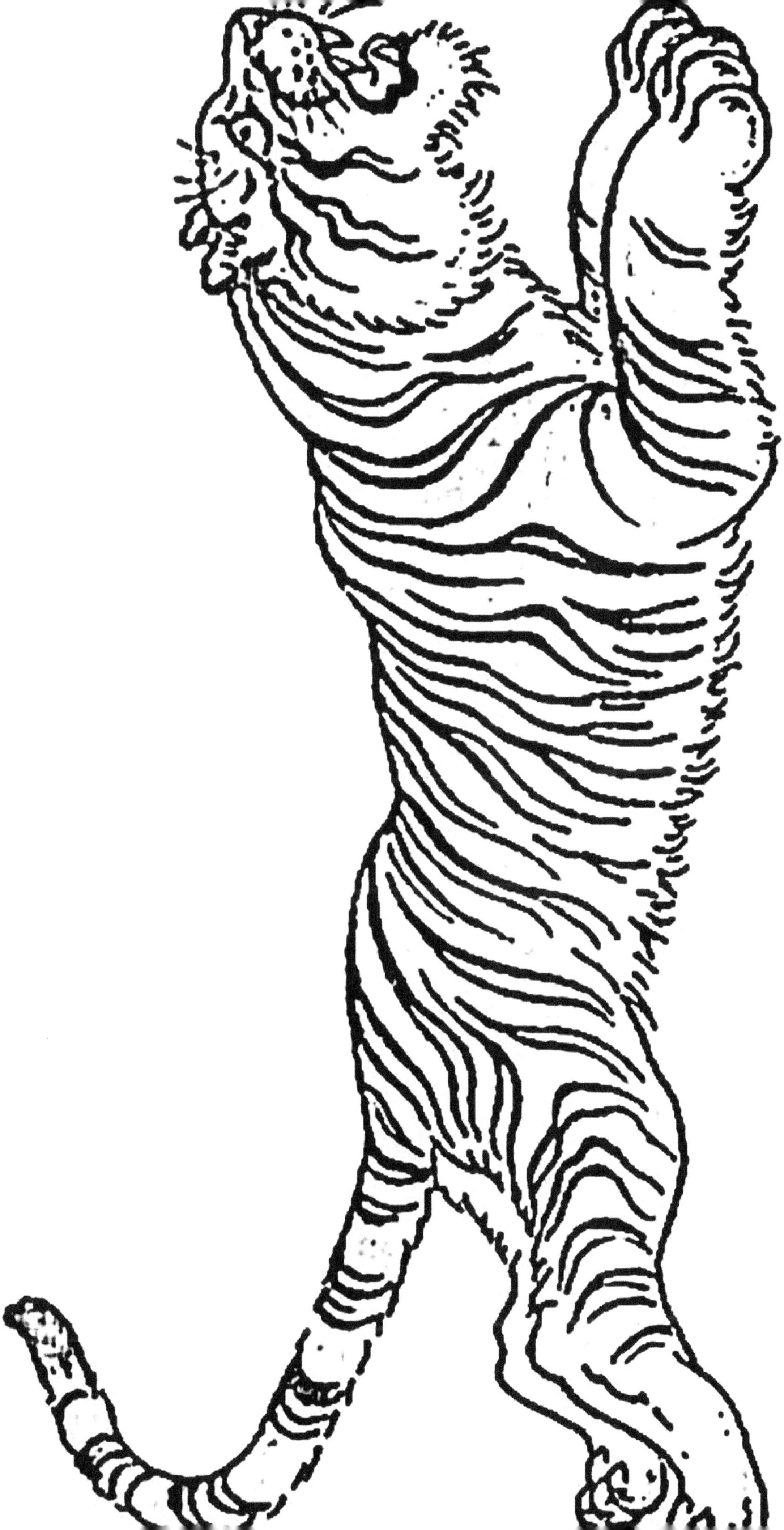

虎

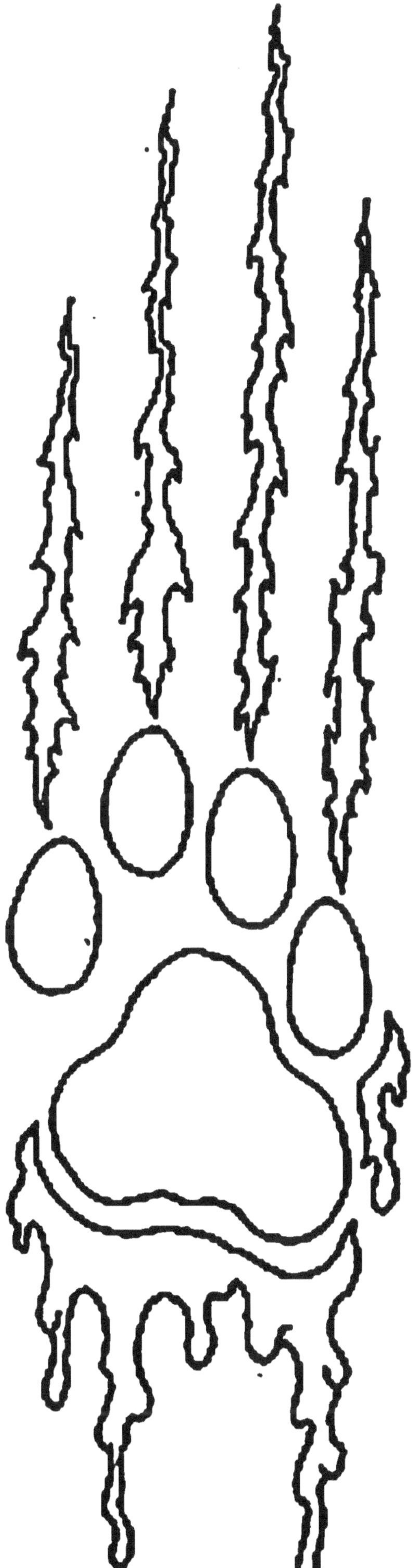

www.ingramcontent.com/pod-product-compliance
Lightning Source LLC
Chambersburg PA
CBHW051949280526
45789CB00009B/3229
* 9 7 8 1 5 3 9 5 4 1 2 8 8 *